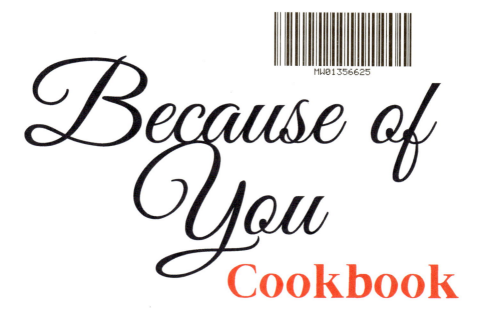

Cookbook

Recipes from the Heart for the Heart

Includes: Personal Journal, Food, Nutrition, and Health Guide

Teen Edition

All rights reserved. No part of this publication may be reproduced, distributed, or transmitted in any form or by any means, including photocopying, recording, or other electronic or mechanical methods, without the prior written permission of the publisher, except in the case of brief quotations embodied in critical reviews and certain other noncommercial uses permitted by copyright law. All pictures are held by commercial license and may not be duplicated by anyone without express permission. Contact: admin@epublishyou.com for inquiries.

ISBN: 13-9798769058851

Although the author and publisher have made every effort to ensure that the information in this book was correct at press time, the author and publisher do not assume and hereby disclaim any liability to any party for any loss, damage, or disruption caused by errors or omissions, whether such errors or omissions result from negligence, accident, or any other cause.

Results commensurate with application and implementation. No guarantees of personal success. As with all information, your success is dependent upon many factors, including you.

Dedication

The "Because of You" cookbook is dedicated to teens and young adults from our hearts to yours. A special thanks to all of those who support, bless, mentor, adopt, foster, protect, provide, and prepare teens without families for a prosperous future, especially those aging out of the foster care system.

"Because of You" is to remember that there is someone in each of our lives that we can say, "Because of You, I can; Because of You, I will; Because of You I did; and Because of You I am." "Because of You" speaks to the words of encouragement, sharing a simple meal, spending time with a young person, giving them a place to call home for the holidays, providing the tools they need for their health, wealth and success.

Finally, this book is dedicated to Mary Johnson who walked into an orphanage and saw me sitting in a corner, picked up the phone and called her husband Freddie and said "we are about to have a little girl."

To Mommy and Daddy, and all of the foster and adopted parents you represent this book is dedicated to you because you gave me the recipe for love, life and success and for that I will be forever grateful. Because of You, there is a Home4Me.

Donna Lee Reed, Founder of Home4Me, "A Voice for Teens in Foster Care"

Home4Me
HOPE | OPPORTUNITIES | MENTORSHIP | EDUCATION

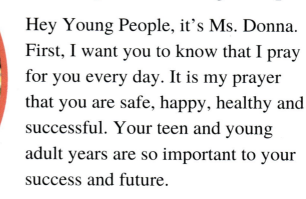

A Message to Young People

Hey Young People, it's Ms. Donna. First, I want you to know that I pray for you every day. It is my prayer that you are safe, happy, healthy and successful. Your teen and young adult years are so important to your success and future.

The healthy and educational choices you make now will ensure you will enjoy a healthy successful lifestyle.

On behalf of those who shared a recipe or made a contribution to this cookbook in any way, we all did it from our hearts to your healthy heart.

For those of you who have experienced the foster care system we want you to know that Home4Me is here for you. I founded the organization Home4Me and designed the LEG up on LIFE program because I grew up in foster care, I understand the need, the importance of belonging and most important because I really care about your health, wealth and success!

BTW my favorite foods are veggie pizza, wraps, collard greens and smoothies.

God Bless You,
Ms. Donna
Ms. Donna

Cool Breezy Tea

Ingredients

2 small cucumbers
6 strawberries
1 cup of mint

2-16oz glasses
24 ounces of water

Directions

Cut cucumbers, strawberries, mint and combine all ingredients with equal amount in each glass add 12 oz of water to each glass.

Sit in refrigerator for at least 30 mins and enjoy.

Tonia Cherry also known as Chef Te' prepares delicious healthy and comfort foods.

Southern Fried Chicken

Ingredients

Chicken wing drummettes (4-6)
Salt & Pepper to taste
¼ tsp Garlic powder
¼ tsp Onion powder
¼ tsp Paprika
1 quart canola oil

Directions

Season chicken with salt and pepper.
Heat oil in cast iron skillet. Keep the dial at medium-high degree. DO NOT OVERHEAT.

In a zip-loc bag: Add remaining ingredients to flour in a and then place chicken in flour. Shake well until all chicken parts are covered with the flour. Shake off excess flour and place in cast iron skillet. Fry chicken until chicken is golden brown and crispy. (Air Fryer is a healthier option to the frying pan)

Drs. Major & Dorothy McGuire: Southern Fried Chicken, from our table to yours. He cooks, she consumes, and they love it together.

They lead the War Room Prayer line. 667-770-1476 access code: 856762#.

Wednesday's at 6:15-7:15am EST

Max Out Veggie Mix

Ingredients

1 cup cut/uncut grape tomatoes
1 cup chopped fresh mushrooms
1 cup diced zucchini
1 cup sliced red onions
1 sliced yellow bell pepper
1 salt & pepper to taste
¾ cup chopped fresh cilantro
¼ cup olive oil

Directions

Add olive oil to pan on medium heat. Add tomatoes, mushrooms zucchini, onions, bell pepper and stir. Continue cooking on low heat add salt and pepper and continue to stir. Once desired tenderness has been acquired, plate and serve.

Helpful Hint: Keep in mind all of your ingredients can be eaten (as is) raw.

Tonia Cherry also known as Chef Te' prepares delicious healthy and comfort foods.

Blackberry Lime Smoothie

Blackberry Lime Smoothie

Ingredients

½ cup unsweetened coconut milk
1 cup fresh blackberries
2 ice cubes
1 tablespoon fresh lime juice
2 tablespoons honey
½ teaspoon grated lime peel

Directions

Combine coconut milk, blackberries, ice, lime juice, honey and lime peel in blender. Blend until smooth.

Serve immediately.

Bishop Wade Ferguson: Founder of The 15th Street Church of God & Community Kitchen' Charlotte, NC is passionate about cooking and feeding the homeless healthy meals every week.

Aunties' Delicious Pancakes

Ingredients

Complete Box Pancake Mix
½ cup blueberries
¼ cup syrup

Directions

Prepare box pancake according to directions on box and add whole blueberries (as shown).

Substitute chopped apples, raisins, cinnamon, or banana if desired.
Heat syrup for a few seconds in the microwave for an *extra* treat.

By Martha Arnold (Auntie)

Food and Pantry Must-Haves

Having the right ingredients on hand will make cooking so much easier. Here is a brief list of things that you can pick up at your local grocery store that will allow you to be prepared when you want to whip up a quick snack, drink or meal.

Cabinet/Pantry

Flour
Sugar
Rice
Beans

Peanut Butter
Tomato Sauce
Crackers
Pancake Mix
Pancake Syrup
Cereal
  (Oatmeal/Grits)

Coffee/Tea
Pasta
Ketchup/Mustard
Broth
Canned Soup

Freezer

Fruits
Veggies
Meats

Counter Top

Bread
Onions
Potatoes

Fresh Fruits
Fresh Veggies

Refrigerator

Butter
Eggs
Milk

Juice
Meats (same day use)

Note: Fresh is the best option for fruits and vegetables. Frozen is a good second options. Pay attention to choices. Pay attention to sodium. Choose less sodium options.

Cucumber Mint Salad

Ingredients

1 large cucumber
½ cup mint leaves
4-5 Roma tomatoes

2 Tbs lime juice
2 Tbs olive oil
Salt & Pepper to taste

Directions

Cut tomatoes, cucumbers, and mint in a large bowl, place to the side.
Prepare dressing by combining lime juice, olive oil, salt and pepper into a small bowl, stir well.
Pour dressing on top of your tomatoes, cucumbers and mint, stir and serve. Enjoy.

Tonia Cherry also known as Chef Te' prepares delicious healthy and comfort foods.

Exercise

How much exercise do I need?
2.5 hours of moderate-intense activity a week with 2 days of muscle-strengthening activity.

Will exercise help me to feel better?
Exercise is known to boost mood, sharpen focus, reduce stress and improve sleep.

It can help to lower risk for type 2 diabetes and control blood pressure.

Here are some creative ways to get in daily exercise:

- Walking the dog
- Swimming
- Playing basketball
- Dancing
- Yoga
- Aerobics
- Gardening
- House cleaning

Rose Squire, Health & Nutrition Coach

Combining moderate exercise with healthy eating habits is great way to lower stress & improve lifestyle.

Blood Pressure

Elevated blood pressure can leave one at risk for kidney disease, stroke, and many other conditions including heart attack.

If you have elevated or high blood pressure limit your intake of sugar and salt (sodium), if you are overweight, lose weight, and if you are a smoker consider quitting.

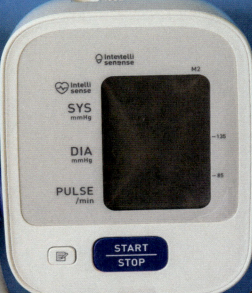

Limit your alcohol intake and do not allow things to stress you out.

Blood pressure measures the force of blood against the arteries when the heart beats and rest. A normal blood pressure is less than 120/80.

Blood pressure lowering foods include: berries, bananas, citrus fruits, spinach, broccoli, avocados, celery, carrots, green leafy vegetables, garlic, salmon.

Homemade Cream of Broccoli Soup

Ingredients
10 oz broccoli stems
4 oz onion (small dice)
2 oz celery (small dice)
1 qt *veloute*
1 cup cream
1½ oz butter
Broccoli florets for garnish

Reagan Gantz: Culinary Student, Livingstone College Foster Care Alumni

Directions

Sweat vegetables in 1½ oz butter. Add 1½ oz flour to make roux. Add chicken stock and let simmer until vegetables are very tender. *Purée* and strain. While straining soup, add cream to your pan and simmer. Heat through.

Blanche brocolli, *shock, d*ry and *sauté* broccoli florets for garnish.

Italicized Terms:

Veloute: (1½ oz flour, 1½ oz butter and 1 qt chicken stock).
Sweat: Allow diced vegetables to release their flavors over low heat.
Purée: Put through a blender and make smooth.
Blanch: Scalding vegetables in boiling water or steam for a short time.
Shock: Plunging just-blanched vegetables into ice water

Caribbean Corned Beef & Cabbage

Ingredients

- 1 can of corned beef
- 1 medium onion
- 1 green bell pepper
- 1 red bell pepper
- 1 head of cabbage
- 4 carrots
- 1 tsp of dried thyme
- 1 tbsp of minced garlic
- 1 tsp of salt
- 1 tsp of black pepper
- 1 tsp of red pepper flakes
- 1 tbsp of ketchup
- ½ cup of olive oil

Directions

Slice the red and green bell peppers into thin slices as well as the onion. Next, you will heat ½ cup of olive oil over medium heat in a deep skillet. Once your oil is heated, sauté green and red peppers and onions for about 3 to 5 minutes or until softened. Add garlic for about a minute more. Add the bag of cole slaw and thyme and let cook for another 10 minutes. Add the corn beef, you will need to break it up in the pot and stir it with the other ingredients and add the ketchup, salt and crushed red pepper flakes, stir and cook for another 3 to 5 minutes.

Serve over rice.

Berneeda Hutchinson, Broad Brook, CT

Loves to cook and bake. Her family has raised several youth in foster care and her heart is in the kitchen making sure everyone is well fed!

Stuffed Baked Garlic & Herb Salt Free Chicken Breast

Ingredients
4 whole chicken breast (skinless)
 2 packs of Knorr chicken flavor broccoli packs
McCormick Salt Free Garlic and Herb seasoning

Directions
Slice chicken breast in half. Season breast with garlic and herb on both sides. Cook rice and broccoli on stovetop 10 minutes. Spray the baking pan with light olive oil or butter spray. Place chicken breast in baking pan one at a time. Fill with rice/broccoli (stuff the breast)
Preheat the oven to 350 degrees and bake for 20-25 minutes (until fully cooked).

Kevin's Kreative Kitchen Korner Recipe
By Kevin Hamilton
Check Kevin out on Youtube Kaptions_Kaught

Salmon Patties

Ingredients

1 -14 ounce cans of Salmon
1 Egg per can of salmon
½ Onion
½ Bell Pepper
½ Cup Flour
Seasoning Chives (optional)
Olive oil or vegetable oil

Directions

Dice your onion and bell pepper, mix together with egg and salmon. (add chives and add to the mix if desired). Put a desirable amount in your hand and roll it around and flatten to a patty. Put some flour on a plate and flour both sides of the patty. Fry or air fry until golden brown. Enjoy and eat with a salad of your choice or on a bun topped with lettuce, tomatoes or with your desired condiments.

Special Health Tip: You can cook the Salmon Patty without the flour.

By Ramone Brian Davis

Carlotta's Vanilla Cupcakes

Ingredients

2 ½ cups all-purpose flour
3 ½ teaspoons baking powder
1 teaspoon salt
1 ¼ cups milk
3 large eggs
1 teaspoon vanilla extract
1 ½ cups white sugar
⅓ cup unsalted butter
¼ cup butter-flavored shortening

Directions

Preheat the oven to 325 degrees. Line two 12-cup muffin tins with cupcake liners.
Sift flour, baking powder, and salt together into a bowl. *Whisk* milk, eggs, and vanilla extract together in a separate bowl.
Beat sugar, butter, and shortening together in a large mixing bowl with an electric mixer until creamy. Mix in flour mixture. Add milk mixture and beat on low speed for 30 seconds. Increase speed to high and beat until smooth, about 2 minutes. Fill the prepared cupcake cups 1/2 full with batter.

Italicized Terms:

Sift: A strainer for separating lumps from powdered material
Whisk: move something or someone very quickly. To beat or mix foods using a special kitchen tool. A fork can be used to whisk.
Ice: To apply icing to cake or cupcake. Icing is thinner than frosting but not quite as thin as a glaze

Lotta Cookies!! & More
"Home of the Build Your Own Cookie!"
LottacookiesNC.com
(FB) Lotta Cookies   (IG) @Lottacookies73

Grilled Peanut Butter & Banana Sandwich

Spread a desired amount of peanut butter on each slice of bread. Take one half of a banana and slice into six pieces. Place the pieces of banana on one side of the bread and then take the other slice of bread and put it on top making a sandwich. Lightly butter each side or put a slice of butter into a small or medium pan.

Place the sandwich inside the pan and cook on medium heat until desired brown on each side.

Tionna Reed's favorite Protein Snack
Tionna is a Culinary Student at Livingstone College.

Carlotta's No Bake Banana Pudding

Ingredients

1 (5 ounce) package instant vanilla pudding mix
2 cups cold milk
1 (14 ounce) can sweetened condensed milk
1 tablespoon vanilla extract
1 (12 ounce) container frozen whipped topping, thawed
1 (16 ounce) package vanilla wafers
14 bananas, sliced
Cherries (optional)

Directions

In a large mixing bowl, beat pudding mix and milk 2 minutes. Blend in condensed milk until smooth. Stir in vanilla and fold in whipped topping. Layer wafers, bananas and pudding mixture in a glass serving bowl. Chill until serving.

Lotta Cookies!! & More
"Home of the Build Your Own Cookie!"
LottacookiesNC.com
(FB) Lotta Cookies   (IG) @Lottacookies73

Peanut Butter Smoothie

Ingredients
1 8oz cup of Almond Milk
1 Banana
 Cup of Ice
2 scoops of oatmeal
2 Heaping Tablespoons of Peanut Butter

(Any brand however, consider natural peanut butter)

Directions
Combine ingredients in blender until all ingredients are combined and smooth.

Ms. Donna's favorite snack.
Donna Lee Reed: Founder of Home4Me

Black Beans & Rice

Ingredients
1 Can Goya Black Bean Soup (low sodium version)
2 cups White Rice (long grain)
2 large onions sliced
1 cup mushrooms (chopped)
1/2 cup cherry tomatoes (cut in half)
1/2 tsp each, garlic powder, onion powder
1 tsp olive oil
1 tbsp olive oil (separately)
Salt & Pepper to taste
Sazon con achiote (achiote is the spice that makes the rice yellow in color.

Directions

In a saucepan, prepare rice according to package directions and add 1/2 packet Sazon and a 1 tsp of olive oil.
In separate saucepan heat black bean soup

In a skillet, add 1 tbsp olive oil, medium heat and add onions. Once onions begin to turn clear, add the mushrooms and cherry tomatoes. Add garlic & onion powder. Salt & Pepper to taste.

Enjoy.

**Lisa Santiago McNeill
Founder, Empowerment Publishing & Multi-Media
Coach | Speaker
IamLisaSantiago.com**

Your Own Recipes

We hope you have enjoyed the recipes included and made them our own. Most of the recipes included are easy to make, simple even. But they were included because they are someone's 'favorite'. Take a moment and write down your favorite. You may even decide to submit it for next year's cookbook.

The LEG up on LIFE Program

LEG up on LIFE Curriculum consists of: coaching, leadership training; personal development; skill and talent development; college prep and educational direction; entrepreneurial and career training; financial literacy; health, wellness and nutrition; independent living skills; preparing youth and young adults to transition from foster care or teen years safely and successfully into society.

This cookbook is one example of some of the preparation our program provides for teens and young people aging out of foster care. You can connect your teen through Home4me.org.

- **Leadership**
  - Confidence
  - Integrity
  - Service - Servant
  - Cultural Awareness & Sensitivity (Understanding others)
  - Accomplishments
  - Communication Skills
- **Entrepreneurship**
  - Skill and Talent Development
  - Business Plan
  - Discover Your Talent i.e Dance, Art, etc.
  - Basic Contracts
  - Negotiation
  - Technology
- **Grooming**
  - Character (who are you in your school, workplace, home)
  - Personal Care/ Personal Hygiene
    - Skin & Skin Care
    - Hair & Hair Care
  - Personal Relationship Building
  - Self Image – Self Esteem
    - Internal & External
    - Fashion

- **Health and Wellness -**
  - Physical, Spiritual, Emotional, Mental
  - Nutrition
    - meal planning
  - Mental and Emotional
    - healing health
    - therapeutic resources for therapy
    - eating right and exercise
- **Personal Development -**
  - Discover Your Purpose
  - Personality Test
  - Identify Accomplishments
  - SWOT –
    Strength - Weakness - Opportunities - Threats

Recipe for Success!!!

Your Vision
Your Voice
Your Value
One Mustard Seed of Faith

Your Vision

Write your Vision in a notebook or journal:

- Write is so plain that when someone reads it they will see just what you see. In other words, make it very plain what your vision is!
- After you write your vision, break it down into achievable goals.
- When you write your goals each one will become the steps you need to take.
- After you have your goal/steps write next to each one when you would like to accomplish each one (realistic short term and long term goals).
- As you begin to take the steps, journal each one and celebrate the big and little achievements.

Your Voice

Understand there is Power of Your Voice

- How you articulate (voice) your vision and who you share it with will be a powerful and important step in achieving what you desire to accomplish.
- Take time and create a few sentences that explain your vision. It's called a Vision Statement.
- Create a mission statement which will explain how you will achieve your vision.
- Speak your Vision and Mission to those who will help you achieve your goals.

Your Value

Understand How Valuable You Are!

- You are so valuable because you have been created for a purpose. Your purpose lines up with your passion. Write what you are passionate about and why you are passionate about it.
- Write down what you can do better than anyone in your circle.
- Ask those you are connected with what they see as your strengths and weaknesses.
- Research how valuable your gifts, talents and skills are. When you have what others need and desire they will pay you for your worth. You just need to know what that is!
- Have Faith that You will Accomplish EVERYTHING you set your MIND to! You've Got This!!!

Donna Lee Reed
Success Coach, Entrepreneur

DonnaLeeReed.com

Empowerment Publishing & Multi-media produces children's books to inspire, uplift and empower our children to greatness. If you have a story that needs to be told that will inspire a child, let us help you to tell it. We offer coaching/publishing packages to suit the beginner and the vet! Our youngest author was only 7 year old! If she can do it, so can you!!

We also publish stories of overcoming, and empowerment, self-help and personal development. Our unique model provides the author with writing support and structuring a business around their book so that they can make the most impact with their story. You lived through it, now use it to EMPOWER others!!

Contacts us at:
author@ePublishYou.com

The EPMM Speakers Bureau can bring authors to your live or virtual event. For more information or to book an event contact the EPMM Speakers Bureau at 704-493-2035 or via email contact: Producers@ePublishYou.com

Lisa Santiago McNeill bringing your story to life. EMPOWERED life!
Coaching, publishing, entrepreneurship.
Lisa@IAmLisaSantiago.com

Made in the USA
Columbia, SC
27 November 2021